JOHANN STRAUSS

Die Fledermaus

[THE BAT]

ENGLISH VERSION
by
RUTH *and* THOMAS MARTIN

ED-2027
ISBN 0-7935-0687-5

G. SCHIRMER, *Inc.*

NOTE

G. SCHIRMER, *Inc.*

42609

CAST OF CHARACTERS

ROSALINDA	**Soprano**
ADELE	**Soprano**
GABRIEL EISENSTEIN	**Tenor**
ALFRED	**Tenor**
DR. BLIND	**Tenor**
DR. FALKE	**Baritone**
FRANK	**Baritone**
SALLY	**Mezzo-Soprano**
FROSCH	**Speaking Part**
PRINCE ORLOFSKY	**Mezzo-Soprano**

Guests at the party, Four Waiters, Chorus

MUSICAL NUMBERS

NO. ACT I PAGE

Overture 2

1. Introduction .... Alfred and Adele 12
Turtle-dove who flew aloft

1a. Duet .... Rosalinda and Adele 16
Ah, my lady says

2. Trio .... Rosalinda, Eisenstein, and Blind 17
When these lawyers don't deliver

3. Duet .... Falke and Eisenstein 28
Come along to the ball

4. Trio .... Rosalinda, Adele, and Eisenstein 35
To part is such sweet sorrow

5. Finale of Act I .... Rosalinda, Alfred, and Frank ....
a. Drinking Song: Drink, my darling 42
b. Couplets: Good sir, are you accusing me 49
c. Trio: No, no, you set my doubts at rest 52

ACT II

6. Entr'acte and Chorus .... Chorus 60
What a joy to be here

7. Couplets .... Prince Orlofsky 65
From time to time I entertain

8. Ensemble and Couplets .. Adele, Orlofsky, Eisenstein, Falke, and Chorus 67
My friends, your kind attention!

9. Duet .... Rosalinda and Eisenstein 74
How engaging, how capricious

10. Csárdás .... Rosalinda 85
Voice of my homeland

11. Finale of Act II .... Principals and Chorus 91
Champagne's delicious bubbles

ACT III

12. Entr'acte 130

13. Melodrama .... Frank 132

14. Couplets .... Adele, Sally, and Frank 136
Ever since I was a baby

15. Trio .... Rosalinda, Alfred, and Eisenstein 143
To judge his expression

16. Finale of Act III .... Full Company 162
Oh, Eisenstein, you master-mind

Die Fledermaus
(The Bat)

C. Haffner and Richard Genée

English version by
Ruth and Thomas Martin

Act I

Johann Strauss

Overture

8
8
p
cresc.
Tempo I
f
Lento
fp
Allegretto
pp
string.

Allegretto
rit.
poco meno
grazioso
f
p
pp
p
poco rit.
cresc.
p
leggiero
poco rit.
a tempo
f
p

Tempo di valse

cre - scen - do molto

staccato

Allegro

Andante

pp p

fp

poco rit.

a tempo

f rit. f

p pp

a tempo

poco rit. f

rit. pp

Allegro moderato
pp
f
mf
ff
fp

G.P.
ff
1
p
G.P.
1
p
Tempo ritenuto
p
pp
pp
rit.
p
p rit.
pp ritard.
fz

Tempo di valse

Più vivo
staccato

No. 1. Introduction

poco rit.
darling Rosalinda, full of ardor is my love, darling Rosalinda!
poco rit
ADELE (entering with an opened letter in her hand)
Allegro
a piacere
Hahahaha
ha
f
Allegretto moderato
This is from my sister
p
rit.
a tempo
(reading)
Sally who belongs to the ballet: "We are going to a
a tempo
rit.
ppp
party which I promise will be gay. Prince Or-

-lof-sky, the talk of the town, will be the host at this su-perb af-fair.
If you're clever you can bor-row one of your la-dy's fan-cy dresses. She has so
poco rit.
a tempo
man-y she won't miss one, and you can't miss a chance like this one. Get the
pp
poco rit.
a tempo
night off, tell a sto-ry, then show up in all your glo-ry. You will see there's nothing
bet-ter!" says my lit-tle sis-ter's let-ter. Much as I would love to
poco ritenuto
poco ritenuto

go, it's not as eas-y as it sounds. If my lady should say no, what would I

cresc.

do? I wish I knew, I wish I knew! Ah!

rit.

Moderato

Could I be that tur-tle-dove

I would soar to clouds a-bove, I could fly to far-off bor-ders, not a soul to

give me or-ders. Why, oh, why did des-ti-ny make a chambermaid of me,

più lento *rit.* *a tempo*

make a chamber-maid ___ of me?

più lento *p* *rit.* *p a tempo*

ADELE:
Oh, my poor, poor aunt!
No. 1a. Duet
Rosalinda and Adele
Moderato
ROSALINDA
ADELE
PIANO
(sobbing)
I'm sor - ry for your aunt, but your request I can - not grant. A trag - ic sit - u - a - tion for your beloved relation. Fate did not do well by you, made a chamber - maid of you.
Ah, my la - dy says I can't go and see my poor, sick aunt. What a trag - ic sit - u - a - tion for my dear be - lov - ed re - la - tion. Why, oh, why did des - ti - ny make a chamber maid of me, make a chamber - maid of me?
più lento
rit.
(exit, weeping)
p rit.
p a tempo
42609

No. 2. Trio

Rosalinda, Eisenstein, and Blind

EISENSTEIN: *Of all the lawyers in Vienna, I had to choose you!*

Let you down? He let you down? *a piacere*

he who let me down! Yes! He's the biggest fool in

Let me down?

Poco mosso

What did he do? What shall I see, explain to me.

town! You soon will see! Lis - ten to

It's n . . not true.

me! How dare you say an - oth - er word? For such a thing there's no ex-

No, first li - li - lis - ten to me!

Don't make a scene! What do you mean?

-plain-ing. My lawyer got me

I be-be-lieve you are complaining!

p

in the soup! You're on-ly talking tom-myrot!

You treat me like a nin-com-poop! Your te-te-tem-per

You drive me ma-ma-mad! You are a

is too hot! You lo-lo-lose your head!

p

char-la-tan!

You are the on-ly one to blame, you

You are no gen-tle-man, you are the on-ly one to blame, you

Why waste your precious voice, you have no oth-er choice!

have a fee-ble scatter-brain!

have a fee-ble scatter-brain!

Meno mosso

(to Blind)

I would suggest you dis-ap-pear, or there will be a scan-dal

Meno mosso

p

here! It would be

I would sug-gest you disap-pear, or there will

it's be-be-best to dis-ap-pear,

best to dis-ap-pear! It would be best to dis-ap-pear! It would be

be a scan-dal here. Yes, go a-way! Get out of here!

to dis-ap-pear! I'll go a-way, away from here!

più lento

best to dis-ap-pear! Be

Get out of here!

(exit)

I'll dis-ap—pear!

Andante mosso
ROSALINDA
calm, my sweet, I beg of you; the court has spo-ken; that is true. With-
dolce
f
p
-in five days, if you sur-ren-der, if you sur-ren-der you can set the matter
rit.
EISENSTEIN
straight! Five days, do you say? Now it is eight! They made my sentence three days
f
long-er! This aw-ful mess is all his fault! This ver-y day I must ap-
f
rit.
a tempo, animato
colla parte
fp
ROSALINDA
That goes too far, I must admit it.
rit.
EISENSTEIN
-pear. If I don't go, they will come here.
You see!

Andante
ROSALINDA
Ah, my dar - ling Ga - bri - el, confined in - side a lone - ly
p
cell, what can I say that will con - sole you? What shall I do with - out
rit.
colla parte
Tempo I
ROSALINDA
you?
EISENSTEIN
f
When these lawyers make a blunder, one is sold right out from un - der. It's e -
f
ROSALINDA
It is real - ly ver - y bad! You are bad!!
EISENSTEIN
- nough to drive me mad. It's e -
BLIND (enters again)
Who is bad?

EISENSTEIN
BLIND
-nough to drive me mad! When your prison term is through, we shall go to court and
sue, then I'll sho-sho-show you all the tricks that I can do.
Un poco agitato
I'm emphatic,
p
p
problematic, a fanatic, I'm asthmatic, I'm magnetic, anaesthetic,
alphabetic, apathetic, I'm pugnacious, disputatious, I'm loquacious,
EISENSTEIN
That's enough! That's e-
BLIND
I'm fallacious, I'm objective, recollective, introspective,
cresc.

ROSALINDA
That's e- nough! that's e- nough! that's e-

EISENSTEIN
-nough!

BLIND
in-ef-fective, I'm pro-li-fic, sci-en-ti-fic,

rit.
-nough! It is e-nough! *a tempo* You may plead and ar- - gue

rit. *a tempo*
You may plead and ar- - gue

rit. *a tempo*
In a word, I'm te-ter-ri-fic. I'm emphatic, problematic,

fz *rit.* *a tempo* *mf*
Ped.

all day long, no mat- - ter what you do, you're

all day long, no mat- - ter what you do, you're

a fanatic, I'm asthmatic, I'm magnetic, anaesthetic, alphabetic,

fz

wrong. You'll nev - er win a sin - gle case, - - ah,
wrong. You'll nev - er win a sin - gle case, - - you'll
apathetic, I'm pugnacious, disputatious, I'm loquatious, I'm fallacious,
fz
Vivace
no, you'll nev - er win a — case. Ah, the way these lawyers
never win a lit - i - ga - tion, win a lit - i - ga - tion. When these lawyers fuss and
recollective, in - effective, su-su-sure, I'll win the case. Why do clients now, I
ff
Vivace
p
blunder, all is lost, it is no wonder! You could real - ly lose your
blun - der, you are sold right out from un - der, you could real - ly lose your
won - der, always bel - low rage, and thunder. You could real - ly lose your

calm! Lose your calm! All he did when he de-fended, was to get his term ex-
calm! Lose your calm! All he did when he de-fended, was to get my term ex-
calm! Lose your calm! All he did when he de-fended, was to get his term ex-
-tended, he a-lone has done the harm, done the harm, done the
-tended, he a-lone has done the harm, done the harm, done the
-tended, he a-lone has done the harm, done the harm, done the
harm, done the harm, done the harm!
harm, done the harm, done the harm!
harm, done the harm, done the harm!

No. 3. Duet

Falke and Eisenstein

FALKE: *Then I can count on you?*
EISENSTEIN: *Well . . .* **Allegretto**

FALKE

PIANO

rit. a tempo

Come a-long to the ball. It will raise your mo-rale!

a tempo rit. p

Jail can wait, why should you wor-ry? There's no need for such a hur-ry, you have time for

one more spree, come and have some fun with me. You will meet the whole bal-

-let, all the pret-ty bal-le-ri-nas, mad'moi-selles and si-gno-ri-nas, they're so

love-ly and pe-tite. My dear fel-low, what a treat, what a treat! With

rit. rit.

blondes and bru - nettes we will dance and dine, and show - er con - fet - ti and

rev - el in wine. In fun and flir - tation the hours will fly, it's one in - vi -

pp

- tation you can't pass by. Ad - mit that a par - ty like this can't

cresc. *p*

fail to put you in shape for your term in_ jail. Do you a -

cresc. *p* *f*

EISENSTEIN

Yes, I a - gree, Yes, I a - gree. ____

FALKE

- gree? Do you a - gree, | Do you a - gree? ____

fz

Andantino

p
But Rosa - lin - da must nev - er know.
Kiss her good - night and off we
pp
go! Say:"Fare you well my pret - ty kit - ten!"
No, no, "my lamb'kin," I shall say "my sweetest
lamb - kin!" While she's sleeping peace - ful - ly I will be the wolf!
rit.
"Sweetest lambkin." While she's sleeping peace - ful - ly you will be the wolf, and
FALKE
a tempo. con moto
un - der the cover of dark, in - stead of to jail, you em - bark with
a tempo, con moto

più cresc.
accelerando
With you on a heavenly lark!
cresc.
accelerando
me on a heav-en-ly lark, with me on a heavenly lark!
cresc.
accelerando
a piacere
I'll present you as a distinguished foreigner. Your name will be Mar-quis Re-
p a tempo
Well, I might be persuaded.
-nard. No one will be one bit the wiser. Say yes! You
But if —
must. Now don't be a cow-ard. You owe it to your-self, old boy!

Animato
You are right, you are right, you're ab-so-lute-ly right!
You really will
Animato
pp
cresc.
Since I'm doing time for an-oth-er crime, I
have a de-light-ful time.
molto cresc.
f
might as well add one more to the list. How can I re-sist? Yes, I'll
You might as well add one more to the list. You'll come then?
cresc.
p
cresc.
Ped.
go with you.
a piacere
This chance is real-ly too good to be
ff

Allegro non troppo

true!—

To a sup-per fit for kings, we shall go with

f *ff* *p*

EISENSTEIN

hearts de-lighted. Lovely wo-men are in-vited, Ev'-ry-bo-dy laughs and sings.

EISENSTEIN

— La la la la la la la la la la la la la la!

FALKE

To a sup-per fit for kings, we shall go with hearts de-lighted.

cresc.

Love-ly wo-men are in-vit-ed, ev'-ry-bo-ly— laughs and sings.—

Love-ly wo- men are in-vit-ed, ev'-ry-bo-dy laughs and sings.

f *f* *mf*

La la la la la
La la la la la la la la la la la la la la la la la la la la la la la la la
p
la la la la la la la la la la la la la la la la la la la la la la la la la
la la la la la la la la la la la la la la la la la la la la la la la la la
f
acceler.
la la la la la la la la la la la la la la la la la la la la la la la la la la la la la la
acceler.
la la la la la la la la la la la la la la la la la la la la la la la la la la
accel. e cresc.
la la la la la la la la.
la la la la la la la.
ff

No. 4. Trio

Rosalinda, Adele, and Eisenstein

ROSALINDA: *Aren't you going to kiss me goodby?*
EISENSTEIN: *Of course.*

Moderato espressivo
ROSALINDA
ADELE
EISENSTEIN
Moderato espressivo
PIANO
mf
p
To part is such sweet
ROSALINDA
sorrow, such pain and such de - spair.
How_ shall I face to - mor - row with -
-out my husband there? With anguish and misgiv - ing
I watch my love de -
part.
How_ can I go on liv-ing? O Lord, it breaks my heart. I dread this
cresc.
poco acceler.
rit.
a tempo
pp
42609

sep - a - ra - tion far more than I can say. I'll live in des - o - la - tion, my

p

cresc. mf

husband gone away. I'll think of you, dear, on - ly, when we are far a - part, and be so ver - y

cresc.

fz

lone - ly, Ah! ——— O Lord, it breaks my

O Lord, it breaks my

EISENSTEIN (sobbing)

fz

O Lord, it breaks my heart! O Lord, it breaks my

p

Allegro moderato

pp

heart! ——— Oh, goodness me, what mis - er - y, how dreadful a ca - lam - i - ty, how

pp

heart! ——— Oh, goodness me, what mis - er - y, how dreadful a ca - lam - i - ty, how

pp

heart! ——— Oh, goodness me, what mis - er - y, how dreadful a ca - lam - i - ty, how

Allegro moderato

pp

dreadful a ca- lam - i - ty, oh, goodness,good - ness me! La la
dreadful a ca- lam - i - ty, oh, goodness,good - ness me! Oh, goodness me,what
dreadful a ca- lam - i - ty, oh, goodness,good - ness me! Oh, goodness me,what
la la la la la la
mis - er - y, how dreadful a ca - lam - i - ty, oh, goodness me,what mis - er - y, oh,
mis - er - y, how dreadful a ca - lam - i - ty, oh, goodness,me,what mis - er - y, oh,
cresc.
Tempo I
Who'll wak - en me each morning to ask me for his socks? Who'll
goodness,gracious!
goodness,gracious!
Tempo I

string.
Meno mosso
dolce
grum - ble for his pa - per, who'll wind the cuckoo clock? And when the night is
cresc.
fall - ing, I get an - other shock. My grief will be ap - pal - - -
agitato
acceler.
Allegro moderato
- ling. Oh, goodness me, what mis- er - y, how dreadful a ca - lam - i - ty, oh, goodness me, what
Oh, goodness me, what mis- er - y, how dreadful a ca - lam - i - ty, oh, goodness me, what
Oh, goodness me, what mis - er - y, how dreadful a ca - lam - i - ty, oh, goodness me, what
Allegro moderato
mis- er - y, oh, goodness, goodness, me! La— la la la—
mis- er - y, oh, goodness, goodness, me! Oh, goodness me, what mis- er - y, how
mis- er - y, oh, goodness, goodness, me! Oh, goodness me, what mis- er - y, how
cresc.

G.P.
la la la la la
dreadful a ca- lam - i - ty, oh, goodness me, what mis- er - y, oh, goodness, gracious!
dreadful a ca- lam- i- ty, oh, goodness me, what mis- er - y, oh, goodness, gracious!
G.P.
EISENSTEIN
What good is all this fretting? There's noth- ing we can
ROSALINDA
ADELE
I find it most up- set-ting! And I feel badly too!
do.
Fare - well, I can't re -
ROSALINDA
ADELE
Fare - well, you can't re - main. Good - bye, good - bye, good - bye,
- main.
Good - bye, goodbye goodbye,

Maestoso
Un- til we meet a- gain, un - til we meet a-
Maestoso
mf
Un- til we meet a- gain. O Lord, it breaks my heart! O
gain, un- til we meet a- gain. O
Un- til we meet a- gain. O Lord, it breaks my heart!
ff
Allegro moderato
pp
Lord, it breaks my heart! Oh, goodness me, what mis - er - y, how dreadful a ca -
Lord, it breaks my heart! Oh, goodness me, what mis - er - y, how dreadful a ca -
O Lord, it breaks my heart! Oh, goodness me, what mis - er - y, how dreadful a ca -
Allegro moderato

-lam - i - ty, oh, goodness me, what mis - er - y, oh, good - ness, gra - cious me! La la
-lam - i - ty, oh, goodness me, what mis- - er - y, oh, good - ness, gra - cious me! Oh, goodness me, what
-lam - i - ty, oh, goodness me, what mis - er - y, oh, good - ness, gra - cious me! Oh, goodness me, what
mf
la la la la la la la
mis- er - y, how dreadful a ca - lam - i - ty, Oh, goodness me, what mis- er - y, oh, goodness, gracious,
mis- er - y, how dreadful a ca - lam - i - ty, Oh, goodness me, what mis- er - y, oh, goodness, gracious.
cresc.
f
la la la
goodness, gra - cious, goodness, gra - cious, goodness, gracious me!
(Eisenstein dances off. Adele follows.)
goodness, gra - cious, goodness, gra - cious, goodness, gracious me!
ff

No. 5. Finale of Act I

(a. Drinking Song, b. Couplets, c. Trio)

ROSALINDA: *That's it,—*
I loved not wisely but too well!

Rosalinda, Alfred, and Frank

Allegretto moderato
ALFRED
ROSALINDA
ALFRED
PIANO
p
Drink, my darling, drink to me!
Drink to all that used to be, To the days we used to know in the ros-y
un poco meno mosso
long a-go. Love is but a fleet-ing dream, nev- er born to last, like a sweet re-
Tempo I
-membered theme from the gold-en past. When your youthful hopes depart,
fz
pp
hopes that brought you hap-piness, Wine will ease your troub-led heart bring for-get-ful-
rit.

a tempo *dolce*

-ness. Night and day, light and gay,

a tempo *p*

let us sing our cares a-way. Night and day, light and gay, we sing our cares a- *rit.*

colla parte

a tempo

-way. Kling, kling, sing, sing, sing, drink with me, sing with me, la la la la la la.

a tempo *più f*

ROSALINDA

Ah, What shall I do! Night and day, *p*

ALFRED

Sing, sing, sing, drink with me, sing, sing, sing, drink with me. Night and day, *p*

p

light and gay, let us drink our cares away! Night and day, light and gay, we *mf*

light and gay, let us drink our cares away! Night and day, light and gay, we *mf*

mf

ril.
a tempo
sing our cares a- way.
rit.
sing our cares a- way.
colle parti
a tempo
ROSALINDA
(to herself)
It's no use what-ev-er, he simply won't go. He'll stay here for-ev-er.
No, no, no, no, no, no, no, no!
ALFRED
Drink on! Drink on! Ah
ALFRED
Drink, my darling, drink to me! Drink to all that used to be. Do not frown so

un poco meno mosso
an-gri-ly. Let me see you smile at me. Once I was your dearest friend,
that is now a dream. But tonight let us pre-tend dreams are what they seem!
Tempo I
Fan-cies bring us happiness, though they soon may pass a-way. Let's believe them
pp
fz
ROSALINDA
Ah! Night and day,
ALFRED
rit.
a tempo
none-the-less, and en-joy to-day. Night and day,
p
light and gay, let us sing our cares away! Night and day, light and gay, we
mf
light and gay, let us sing our cares away! Night and day, light and gay, we
8

rit.
a tempo
sing our cares a - way!
rit.
sing our cares a - way!
colle parti
f a tempo
Marziale (spoken)
(to Alfred)
ROSALINDA: I hear voices, some one is talking! Heavens!
Listen, they are coming
p
p
up the stairs!
ALFRED:
Let them.
ROSALINDA
Heavens! What a situation!
FRANK: (opens the door
and speaks off-stage)
Wait for me outside.
(enters) Do not be shocked, Madame, I am Prison Warden Frank and cannot
resist the pleasure of coming personally to escort
your recalcitrant husband into enforced seclusion.
ROSALINDA: (confused)
But my husband is . . .

Tempo I
ALFRED
ROSALINDA: Please be still, we are not alone.
Drink my dar-ling, drink to me! Drink to all that used to be.
ALFRED: Let us pretend we are.
ALFRED
Kling, kling, sing, sing sing, drink with me, sing with me!
dolce
FRANK: My carriage is waiting below, and I hope you will offer no further resistance.
ALFRED
No. Night and day, light and gay, let us sing our
pp
FRANK: Ha ha ha! Right you are. I see you take the affair from the humorous side.
cares away!
pp
ALFRED (offering Frank a glass):
cresc.
Drink with me, sing with me, sing, sing, sing!
FRANK (spoken) Ha ha ha!
cresc.

ALFRED
mf
Night and day, light and gay, let us sing our cares a - way! Night and day,
f
FRANK
mf
Night and day, light and gay, let us sing our cares a - way! Night and day,
f
8
p
mf
light and gay, we sing our cares a - way!
rit.
light and gay, we sing our cares a - way!
rit.
A
8
rit.
ff a tempo
ROSALINDA (to herself)
What shall I
FRANK
joke in its place is ve - ry fine. Now come with me, dear Mister Eisenstein.
p
ROSALINDA
do, where shall I go?
Più animato
ALFR.
f
I am not your dear Eisenstein, I'm not he, let me tell you...
FRANK
f
You are not
mf
f

ALFRED
The dev-il, no!
ROSALINDA (to Alfred)
For heaven's sake, say that you are!
FRANK
he?
Come, come, be more civ-il!
(to himself)
I wonder what's be-hind all this?
1. Good
b. Couplets
Allegretto moderato
sir, are you ac-cus-ing me of an-y im-pro-pri-e-ty?
That would be quite ab-surd.
How can you think so ill of me to
(2.) night, when he's at home with me, he always dines in-for-mal-ly
in dressinggown and cap.
This in-timate, do-mes-tic scene has

question my in - te - gri - ty, and doubt a lady's word? Does the
always been his set routine be - fore his evening nap. See him
sit - u - a - tion here not ap - pear to be quite clear? What
yawn and nod his head. How he longs to go to bed! What
p
pp
Tempo di Valse, Moderato
man would dare to stay right there, and have a tête - à - tête at half past
man would wear so free an air in an - y la - dy's house, so un - im -
eight in such a state, except my one and le - gal mate,
ALF. -pressed and self possessed, except my one and on - ly spouse.
1. What man would dare to
2. What man would wear so
FRANK
1. What man would
2. What man would
cresc.
pp

ROS.
And have a tête-à-tête at half past eight, in
In an-y la-dy's house, so un-im-pressed, and
ALF.
stay right there and have a tête-à-tête at half past eight
free an air in an-y la-dy's house, so un-im-pressed
FR.
stay right there, and have a tête-à-tête at half past eight
wear an air in an-y la-dy's house, so un-im-pressed,
cresc.
such a state, ex-cept my one and le-gal mate.
self-pos-sessed, ex-cept my one and on-ly.
in such a state, ex-cept her one and le-gal mate.
and self possessed, ex-cept her one and on-ly.
in such a state, ex-cept her one and le-gal mate.
and self possessed, ex-cept her one and on-ly.
mf
ff
f
1.
2.
ROSALINDA
FRANK
a3
2. At spouse.
No,
Tempo I
p
pp
ff
p

c. Trio
Allegro non troppo
FRANK
no, you set my doubts at rest, I'm sure you did not lie. But
come, dear Mis - ter Ei - sen - stein, and kiss your wife good - bye.
cresc.
ROSALINDA
Kiss me good - bye?
p
riten. a piacere
Well then, if you in - sist. Now there you have the
ALFRED
Kiss her goodbye!
FRANK
Kiss her good - bye!
fz
Vivace con fuoco
kiss!
poco rit.
Tempo I
ALFRED
Since I have no - bly ris - en to live your husband's life of
p

ALFRED
pp ritard.
crime, before I go to pris-on, come, kiss me just one more time!
FRANK
f
E-
espress.
ritard.
FRANK
-nough! I must be on my way, for I must go to a soi-rée. Let's leave without de-lay, so
fz
p
cresc.
f
ROSALINDA
(softly to Alf.)
Allegretto
You surely will meet my husband as
let us leave without de- lay!
(goes toward the door, opens it, and gives a sign to the policeman outside)
fp
p dolce
ROSALINDA
well.
Be still, I im-plore!
ALFRED
Per-haps we shall be in the very same cell.
You may be
cresc.

Allegretto
Be still, I im - plore!
Ah!
sure!
You may be sure!
FRANK
Down there at the gate, my horse and carriage
Allegretto
mf
FRANK
wait. So come, we shall be late. My lovely, lively pigeonhouse is
p
nice as it can be. The birds who flutter in and out get food and lod - ging
free. I just have one more va - can - cy, a co - zy lit - tle nest; if
cresc.

you will kindly come with me, it will be yours im-me-diately. Don't miss this op-por-
ALFRED
tu-ni-ty to be my honored guest. If it must be then I shall
ROSALINDA
Do it for me!
go. Then be it so.
FRANK
Come
ALFRED
I'll go but not be-fore — I've kissed my wife once
on! Let's go!

n poco meno
ROSAL.
Enough, my friend, now please be - have!
No, no, e -
ALFRED
more.
Anoth- er kiss will make me brave.
espress.
Un poco meno
mf
- nough, you must be go - ing.
rit.
One last kiss and then I'll be forti - fied.
rit.
Più moto
FRANK
Enough do - mest - ic bliss, my friend, or there will nev-er be an end, e -
mf
f
ROSALINDA
a tempo
p
His love - ly, lively pigeon-house is
ALFRED
p
His love - ly, lively pigeon-house is
FRANK
- nough, e - nough, my friend!
p
My love - ly, lively pigeon-house is
a tempo
p

mf
nice as it can be. The birds who flutter in and out get food and lodging free. — He
nice as it can be. The birds who flutter in and out get food and lodging free. — He
nice as it can be. The birds who flutter in and out get food and lodging free. — I
just has one more va-can-cy, a co-zy lit-tle nest, it is an op-por-
just has one more va-can-cy, a co-zy lit-tle nest; it is an op-por-
just have one more va-can-cy, a co-zy lit-tle nest; don't miss the op-por-
f
-tu-ni-ty to be his honored guest. Yes, yes,
-tu-ni-ty to be his honored guest. I_ yield for now and
tu-ni-ty to be my honored guest. I beg you, kind-ly
42609

Listesso tempo
fol - low him to be his honored guest. Go with
fol - low him to be his hon - ored guest. I shall
fol - low me, I beg you, kind - ly follow me, kind - ly
him for my sake. Ah yes you'll help me out of this unpleasant
go for your sake. Why did he dis-turb this pleasant
follow me right a - way. Come, because I did ac - cept an
fz p
sit - u - a - tion, yes, my friend, you must do this for me. Ah,
sit - u - a - tion? Did he have to come and call for me? Ah,
in - vi - ta - tion, come, I beg you, come at once with me.
f

yes, you'll help me out of this unpleas-ant sit-u-a-tion, go, ah,
yes, why why did he dis-turb this pleas-ant sit-u-a-tion, ah, for
Come, because I did ac-cept an in-vi-ta-tion, come with
fz
go with him, it must be so.
now it must be so, it is to
me, come with me, it must be, it must be. Ah!
ff
Meno ad libit.
a tempo
Ah, it must be so. Ah!
be, it must be so. Ah! (Alfred is led away by Frank. Curtain)
yes, it must be so. Ah, come!
fz
ff

End of Act I

Act II

No. 6. Entr'acte and Chorus

-ca-sion. So u-nique, so de-lightful, it's the par-ty of the year!
-ca-sion. So u-nique, so de-lightful, it's the par-ty of the year!
-ca-sion. So u-nique, so de-lightful, it's the par-ty of the year!
Nothing could be more in-triguing than this most en-chanting at-mosphere.
Nothing could be more in-triguing than this most en-chanting at-mosphere.
most en-chanting at-mosphere.
Let us all be hap-py while we may, we still are young and gay. For to-
Let us all be hap-py while we may, we still are young and gay.
we are young and gay.

pp poco riten.
a tempo
-day, let's be gay, let's be gay, let's be gay, let's be gay! We will dance, we will
pp
f
Let's be gay, let's all be gay! We will dance, we will
pp
f
Let's all be gay! We will dance, we will
f
p poco riten.
f a tempo
sing, we will have a cel-e- bra-tion. With a song and with laughter let us
sing, we will have a cel-e- bra-tion. With a song and with laughter let us
sing, we will have a cel-e- bra-tion. With a song and with laughter let us
p
f
p
Molto animato
SOPRANO I
make the raft-ers ring.
Please bring some to-
1st WAITER
make the raft-ers ring.
Hors d'oeuvres!
make the raft-ers ring.
Molto animato
f p

SOPRANO II
SOPRANO III
me!
One right here for me!
Here!
2ND WAITER
Cherry Brandy!
3RD WAITER
Turkish candy!
4TH WAITER
Sacher-
SOPRANO IV
SOPRANO V
SOPRANO VI
Please!
I'll have a cup of tea!
And coffee here for me!
THE WAITERS
-tor-te!
At
SEVERAL WOMEN
Coffee here!
SEVERAL MEN
once! At once!
Bring us beer!
accelerando
Vivo.
TUTTI
The golden moments swiftly pass, we must enjoy them while we may, So

laugh and sing and fill your glass, For to - day, let us play, let us play the night a -
laugh and sing and fill your glass, For to - day, let us play, let us play the night a -
laugh and sing and fill your glass, For to - day, let us play, let us play the night a -
-way, For all too soon the mo - ments pass, Let us sing, let us play, let us
-way, For all too soon the mo - ments pass, Let us sing, let us play, let us
-way, For all too soon the mo - ments pass, Let us sing, let us play, let us
dance the night a - way. Let's be gay! Let's be gay!
dance the night a - way. Let's be gay! Let's be gay!
dance the night a - way. Let's be gay! Let's be gay!

No. 7. Couplets

Prince Orlofsky

ORLOFSKY: *Now let me acquaint you with the rules of my house!*
Allegro non troppo
ORLOFSKY
PIANO
p
p marcato
1. From time to time I entertain, I am the perfect host. My guests drink vod-ka and champagne, and do what they like most. Each one is free to have his fun, my house is free-dom hall. In oth er words, to coin a pun: It is a free-for-all. You're
2. There's not_ a sight I have not seen, no place I have not been. There's not a thing be-neath the sun I have-n't heard or done. There's not a price I can-not pay, no sum I can't af-ford, But I have nev-er found a way to keep from be-ing bored I
poco meno
poco meno

marcato
free to go and free to — come, you're free to go a - stray. I want you to en -
do not care for mu - sic — much, not e - ven Jo - hann Strauss. The op - er - et - ta
p marcato
- joy your self, but don't get - in my way. I want you to en - joy yourself, but
I hate — most is called "Die Fle - der - maus," The op - - er - et - ta I hate — most is
don't get — in my way — And if it — does not suit you, that too, is up to
called "Die Fle - der - maus." — If — you don't like it ei - ther, you know what you can
pp
poco rit.
a tempo
you, that too, is — up to — you. We — Rus - sians have a mot - to: Cha - cun à son goût, We —
do, you know what you can do: Get — up and leave the theater: Cha - cun a son goût, Get —
a tempo
poco rit.
cresc.
1.
2.
Russians have a motto: Chacun à son goût.
up and leave the theater: Chacun a son goût.
1.
Dialogue
2.
cresc.

No. 8. Ensemble and Couplets

Adele, Orlofsky, Eisenstein, Falke, and Chorus

Un poco meno mosso
ORLOFSKY
See this de - light - ful la - dy, Marquis Re - nard takes her for . . no, I
p
4 SOPRANOS
FALKE
ADELE
can't be - lieve it . . For what then? Take a guess! He takes me for a
chambermaid on hol - i - day par - ade.
Più animato
ORLOFSKY WITH SOPRANOS
mf
Ha ha ha ha ha ha ha
TUTTI
FALKE WITH TENOR II
Ha ha ha ha
Più animato
Ha ha ha ha
cresc.
ha ha ha,
ha, He's try - ing to be fun - ny, ha ha ha ha ha ha ha!
ha ha, He's try - ing to be fun - ny, ha ha ha ha ha ha ha!
ha ha, He's try - ing to be fun - ny, ha ha ha ha ha ha ha!
f
rit.

Meno
ORLOFSKY
Marquis, you are most im-po-lite, you sure-ly are mistaken! How im-po-
crescendo
-lite!
FALKE
How im-po- lite!
EISENSTEIN
The like-ness was a shock to me!
How im- po- lite!
TUTTI
How im- po- lite!
How im-po-
How im- po- lite!
How im-po-
p
grazioso
EISENSTEIN
I could have sworn that it was she!
How im-po-lite!
-lite!
-lite!
p
rit.

Allegretto
ADELE
1. My dear Marquis, it seems to me you should dis - play more tact!
2. Just look at me and you will see there's more than meets the eye.
Allegretto
pp
leggiero
Where a la - dy goes, what a la - dy shows, is how she
Where a la - dy's been, where a la - dy's seen, are proofs that
proves the fact! My taste is too fine and too chic, ah My
nev - er lie. Could I be at home in this room, ah If
legg.
waist has a line too u - nique, ah. My talk is too dra - ma - tic, my
I were at home with a broom, ah. The way I lift an eye - brow is
cresc.

rit.
a tempo
walk a-ris-to- crat-ic. What chambermaid you know could have so much to show, what
ty-pic-al-ly highbrow! What chambermaid you know could have so much to show, what
mf
cham-bermaid you know could have so much to show? In-stead of put-ting
cham-bermaid you know could have so much to show? You might as well ad-
pp
cresc. e rit.
p a tempo
on such airs, why don't you mind your own af-fairs? It's too fun-ny, ha ha ha,
-mit, Mar-quis, you owe me an a-pol-o-gy. It's too fun-ny, ha ha ha,
a tempo
cresc. e rit.
p
Please excuse me, ha ha ha, I can't help it, ha ha ha, You amuse me, ha ha ha ha ha ha.
Please excuse me, ha ha ha, I can't help it, ha ha ha, You amuse me, ha ha ha ha ha ha.

ADELE
It's too fun - ny, ha ha ha, Please ex - cuse me, ha ha ha ha,
CHORUS
It's too fun - ny, ha ha ha, Please ex - cuse me, ha ha ha ha ha ha
It's too fun - ny, ha ha ha, Please ex - cuse me, ha ha ha ha ha ha
It's too fun - ny, ha ha ha, Please ex - cuse me, ha ha ha ha ha ha.
cresc.
ha ha You're wrong as you can be, Mar -
ha ha ha ha ha ha ha!
ha ha ha ha ha ha ha!
ha ha ha ha ha ha ha!
1.
p
colla parte
sfp
quis
f a tempo
p

2.
Ah!
2.
p
f
Ha ha ha ha ha
Ha ha ha ha ha
Ha ha ha ha ha
Più mosso
ha!
ha!
ha!
ff

No. 9. Duet

Rosalinda and Eisenstein

stringendo
wait, dear Ei-sen-stein. I will make you toe the line, I will make you toe the
stringendo
line.
a tempo
Like a fleet-ing, mag-ic vi-sion, you may van-ish from my sight! Will you
a tempo
Allegro
Please, my dear Mar-
rit.
change your firm de-ci-sion and unmask for me to-night?
Allegro
rit.
p
pp
rit.
-quis, don't ask me. That's the one thing I won't do. I in-sist you don't un-
rit.

Tempo I
a tempo
(to herself)
-mask me. I ex-pect that much from you.
How he prances and ro-
(to himself)
From her glances
più rit.
a tempo
f
fz
p
-man-ces while he bold-ly makes ad-van-ces. No sus-pi-cion, pre-mon-
and ad-van-ces I have chances, I am sure. If I try
-i-tion, warns him who re- sists his charms. In a min-ute he'll dis-
and per-sist, how can she re-sist? In a min-ute
mf
poco rit.
-cov-er, this phi-land- - - 'ring, would-be lov-er, how com-
poco rit.
I'll dis-cov-er, yes, I will see. wheth-er she can re-
f
poco rit.

dolce riten. a tempo

-plete-ly he has fal-len in my trap! ——

dolce riten.

-sist, or will fall in-to my trap. ——

a tempo

colle parti

p *pp*

Moderato **Meno**

ROSALINDA (with weak voice, placing her hand upon her heart and staggering to the couch)

Ah, my heart is weak and tender, and my brain be-

Moderato **Meno**

pp *pp*

-gins to spin.

EISENSTEIN (observing her triumphantly)

f

Ah, ——she's going to sur-ren-der, pretty soon she will give

fz *p*

Ped. *

(as before)

Ah, my pulse is beat-ing wild-ly, throbbing on, tick, tock, tick, tock! Could we

in.

mea - sure its pul - sa - tions by your pre - cious lit - tle clock?
That's just
what I want to say!
Let us count them right a - way!
cresc.
cresc. molto
Yes, let us count, yes, let us count, yes, let us count them right a -
Yes, let us count, let us count, let us count them right a -
poco rit.
dolce
Allegro
- way.
- way.
One,
pp
p

five, six, sev'n, nine,

two, three, four, No, that's not in

Più lento

I thought per haps that I was

line, for af - ter sev - en there is eight.

Più lento

p

a piacere

late, let's change po - si - tions. You count the beats of my

Change them? How?

colla parte

(she takes watch and chain, which Eisenstein hands her)

heart, and I the ticking of your watch, and let us start from the start.

Più Allegro
Now let us count without de-lay.
Yes, right a-way.
Più Allegro
p
animato
One, two, three, four, five, six, sev'n, eight, nine, ten, 'leven, twelve, thirteen, fourteen,
One, two, three, four, five, six, sev'n, eight, hop, hop, hop, hop, on with-out a
pp animato
fif-teen, sixteen, sev'nteen, eighteen, nineteen, twenty, thirty, for-ty,
stop! One, two, three, four, five, six, ten,
f
p
fif-ty, six-ty, eighty, hun-dred. My good-ness, we
hop, hop, hop, hop, with-out stop, six hundred and nine!
f
sfp

can't be that far!
No,
no,
Oh, yes, in- deed, we are,
half a
mil- lion beats, at
no!
That is a lit- tle too fan-
least,
yes, half a mil - lion beats, at least!
(putting the watch in her pocket)
poco rit.
- tas - tic!
You'll nev- er count
an- oth- er
My fig - ures are a bit e - las - tic.
poco rit.
a tempo
heartbeat.
I
She took my watch a-way from me, how un-kind!
a tempo

rit.
thank you sin-cere-ly! I'll cher-ish it dear-ly.
If you don't mind?
rit.
Poco meno
p
Ah,
Poco meno
p
p
She out- wit- ted all my guess-es,
and my watch she now pos-sess-es. This flir-ta-tion cost me dear-ly,

(laughing)
Ah,
(grasping for the watch)
I disgraced my-self se-vere-ly. Ah! Lovely watch, oh, give it back!
pp
Ah,
rit.
Please, give it back!
rit.
a tempo
Ah,
p
I dis-graced my- self se- vere- - ly. Ah, dearest watch, if I
a tempo
p
on-ly had you back! Please give it back!
cresc.

pp
Più mosso
f
Ah,
pp
f
This flir - ta - tion cost me dearly; I disgraced myself severely! And my watch has
Più mosso
pp
f
Ah,
Ah
gone to waste. Ah, I am dis - graced. Poor
fz
f
p
Allegro molto
Ah!
me!
Allegro molto
f
ff
fz
Ped.
fz

No. 10. Csárdás

Rosalinda

ROSALINDA: *The melodies of my homeland will speak for me!*

Langsam (Slow)
PIANO
fp
ROSALINDA
mf
Voice of — my homeland, nos - tal - gic, enthralling, I — hear you cal · ling and tears fill my eyes. —
p
f
accel.
a tempo
Dreaming, I — hear — your — plain -tive sigh - ing, and — I'm lone - ly for — you, my na - — tive — skies. O
cresc.
colla voce
pp

home-land I hold so dear, where sun-light is
golden and clear, where green forests tow-er, and fields are in flow-er. O
accel.
cresc.
accel.
f
land that I love and revere. Nev-er, oh, nev-er your
rit.
p
a tempo
accel.
im-age will fade from my mem-o-ry,
a tempo
poco rit.
rit.
pp
your be-lov-ed name! wherev-er I may wander, Ah!
f
fz

far. Ah. As lone-ly years go
accel. lento a piacere
by, to you my thoughts will fly, till the
accel. fz lento fz pp
a tempo
day I die! O home-land I hold so dear, where
a tempo
pp
sun-light is gold- en and clear, where green forests tow-er, and
accel. f p rit. a tempo
fields are in flow-er, O land that I love and revere!
a tempo
accel. f p rit.

Friszka
Fie- ry_ evening sky, spir- its are soaring high. Friends all_
gath-er round, hear the Csárdás sound. Love- ly_gyp-sy girl, come, dance the
mer-ry whirl; child of_ Ro-ma-ny, give your heart to me!
glissando
Fid-dles are ring- ing,_ hey_ ya, wild- ly
gliss.
a tempo
sing- ing,_ hey_ ya!_ ha!
Twirl- ing round and round, stamping the
a tempo
p
mf

dus - ty ground, dance the night a - way till the break of day. Lads and
lass - es, lift your glass - es, pass the bot - tles, pass the
bot - tles fast from hand to hand! Drown your sor - row till to -
mor - row. Raise a toast to the fath - er - land! ha!
rit.

a tempo
Fie - ry eve - ning sky, spir - its are soaring high. Friends all
a tempo
p
gath - er round, hear the Csárdás sound.
Più Allegro
La la la la
p
la la la la la la la la
la la la
f
Lento
Allegro
ff
la la la la la!
ff
ff
ff

No. 11. Finale of Act II

Principals and Chorus

EISENSTEIN: ... *A toast to the life of our party, — to King Champagne!*

Allegro con brio
ORLOFSKY
1. Champagne's de - li - cious bub - bles, tra -
EISENSTEIN.
2. pagne is so ma - jes - tic, tra -
ADELE
3. pagne is so ro - man - tic, tra -
Allegro con brio
PIANO
la la la la la la la, scat - ter all our troub - les tra - la la la la la
la la la la la la la, for - eign and do - mes - tic, tra - la la la la la
la la la la la la la, glo - rious and gi - gan - tic, tra - la la la la la
O. 1. la. It mel - lows pol - i - ti - cians and bet - ters world con - di - tions. All
E. 2. la. It makes the world we live in, a bet - ter place to give in! All
A. 3. la. It makes the world look thrill - ing, and men be - come more will - ing! All

a 3
1. dip - lo - mats and rul - ers should keep it in their cool - ers.
2 "good and jol - ly fel - lers" should keep it in their cel - lars. We toast cham -
3. girls who long for sa - bles, should keep it on their ta - bles.
pagne, the es - sence of the es - sence, the King of Ef - fer - ves - cence, the
King of Ef - fer - ves - cence! A toast, a toast, a toast! His
CHORUS
ROSALINDA AND SALLY WITH SOPRANO
A toast, a toast, a toast!
FRANK WITH TENOR
A toast, a toast, a toast!
FALKE WITH BASS
A toast, a toast, a toast!
(a 8)
maj - es - ty we cel - e - brate, cel - e - brate, long and late, joyous - ly to - gether. We toast Champagne, the

ROSALINDA, ADELE, ORLOFSKY
Great! His majesty we cel-ebrate, celebrate, long and late, Joyous-ly to-gether.
EISENSTEIN
His majesty we cel-ebrate, celebrate, long and late, Joyous-ly we drink to Cham
SALLY WITH SOPRANO I
His majesty we cel-ebrate, celebrate, long and late, Joyous-ly we drink to Cham-
FRANK WITH TENOR II
His majesty we cel-ebrate, celebrate, long and late, Joyous-ly we drink to Cham-
FALKE WITH BASS
His majes-ty we cel-ebrate, celebrate; long and late, Joyous-ly we drink to Cham-
CHORUS
mf
1. and 2.
Ah, the Great! A toast to Champagne, the great monarch.
EISENSTEIN
2. Cham-
-pagne, the Great! A toast to Champagne, the great monarch.
ADELE
3. Cham-
-pagne, the Great! A toast to Champagne, the great monarch..
-pagne, the Great! A toast to Champagne, the great monarch.
-pagne, the Great! A toast to Champagne, the great monarch.
1. and 2.
f
p

3

Ah, — the Great!

-pagne, — the Great!

-pagne, — the Great!

-pagne, — the Great!

-pagne, — the Great!

3.

ff

Un poco moderato

f

p

EISENSTEIN

My Chev-a-lier, oh, bon a-mi!

FRANK

Mer-ci, merci, mer-ci! An-

-oth-er little drink, Mar-quis!

EISENSTEIN

Oui, oui, oui, oui, oui oui!

ROSALINDA, ADELE
SALLY, ORLOFSKY
Ha ha ha, Tou-
EISENSTEIN, FRANK
Tou-ché, tou-ché tou-ché!
FALKE
That's enough of French for to-day.
Tou-
CHORUS
(All laughing)
Tou-
Tou-
Tou-
ROSALINDA, ADELE
SAL., ORL.
-ché, tou-ché, touché!
FALKE
-ché, tou-ché touché! Friends gather near. Here's my i-dea!
I
-ché, tou-ché touché!
Let us hear!
-ché, tou-ché, touché!
Let us hear!
-ché, tou-ché, touché!
Let us hear!

see that hap - py couples are meeting, that many hearts with true love are beating; So
why not con - ti - nue in this hap - py mood and sing to love and bro - ther -
rit.
ORLOFSKY
- hood! I a - gree most heart - i - ly, that's good.
CHORUS
Let us sing to love and bro - ther -
Let us sing to love and bro - ther -
Let us sing to love and bro - ther -
EISENSTEIN (to Rosal.)
ROSALINDA
-hood! You, too, love - ly la - dy, must be there. When all are kiss - ing, I
-hood!
-hood!

FALKE
can't be missing. Let's lift our glas-ses and drink a-gain, and ev-'ry-bod-y
join the refrain.
cresc.
Allegretto moderato
Sing to love, love we nev-er knew be-fore,
May it flourish and bloom for ev-er-more, Sing to love, ev-erlast-ing
hap-pi-ness, let us all be friends to-geth-er. For e-

-ter - ni - ty, a fra - ter - ni - ty of com - pan - ions,
friends, and lov ers.
rit.
p rit.
Poco più animato
First one kiss,
then one more, you, you, and al - ways you!
You kiss me, I kiss you, you,
f
you, on - ly you, on - ly you, on - ly, on - ly
decresc. poco rit.
tr
p
poco rit.

Tempo I (Allegretto moderato)

ORLOFSKY

Sing to love, — love we nev-er knew be - fore, — May it flour - ish and

EISENSTEIN

Sing to love, — love we nev - er knew be - fore, —

FALKE

you!

FALKE, FRANK

Sing to love, —

Tempo I. (Allegretto moderato.)

mf

ROSALINDA

Sing to love, — love we nev - er knew be - fore,

ADELE, SALLY

Sing to love, —

ORLOFSKY

bloom for ev - er - more. Let us —

EISENSTEIN

May it flour - ish for ev - er - more,

FALKE, FRANK

— love we nev-er knew be - fore, — May it flour - ish for

ROSALINDA
let us all be friends, let us_ all, let us all_ be friends to-
ADELE, SALLY
— love we nev-er knew be-fore, ._ let us all_ be friends to-
ORLOFSKY
all be friends,_ let us all_ be friends to-
EISENSTEIN
ev- er- more._ Let us sing,_ let us sing,_
FALKE, FRANK
ev- er- more, for ev- er-
6 SOPRANOS
Yes, join
2 TENORS
Let us sing,_ let us sing,_
2 BASSES
Join
CHORUS

pp
-geth - er. For e - ter - ni - ty, a fra - ter - ni - ty!
-geth - er. For e - ter - ni - ty, a fra - ter - ni - ty!
-geth - er. For e - ter - ni - ty, a fra - ter - ni - ty!
— let us sing! — For e - ter - ni - ty, a fra -
-more. For e - ter - ni - ty, a fra -
in! For e - ter - ni - ty, a fra - ter - ni - ty!
— let us sing! — For e - ter - ni - ty, a fra -
in! For e - ter - ni - ty, a fra -
p
Join in, join in, join in,
Join in, join in, join in,
Join in, join in, join in,

Animato
cresc.
rit.
p
Let us all be friends to - gether. First one kiss,
Let us all be friends to - gether. First one kiss,
Let us all be friends to - gether. First one kiss,
-ni - ty! Let's all be friends to - gether. First one kiss,
-ter - ni - ty. Let us all be friends to - geth - er. First one kiss,
Let us all be friends to - gether. First one kiss,
-ter - ni - ty. Let's all be friends to - gether. First one kiss,
-ter - ni - ty. Let us all be friends to - geth - er. First one kiss,
join in, join in, join in, yes, join all in!
join in. join in, join in, yes, join all in!
join in, join in, join in, yes, join all in!
Animato
ritard.
p

then one more, you, you, you, on - ly you!–
then one more, you, you, you, on - ly you!–
then one more, you, you, you, on - ly you!
then one more, you, you, you, on - ly you!
then one more, you, you, you, on - ly you!
then one more, you, you, you, on - ly you!–
then one more, you, you, you, on - ly you!
then one more, you, you, you, on - ly you!
First one kiss, then one more, you, you, you, you, you, you, you, you,
First one kiss, then one more, you, you, you, you, you, you, you, you,
First one kiss, then one more, you, you, you, you, you, you, you, you,
decresc.

pp
molto cresc.
ff
First one kiss, then one more, kiss me, kiss me,
cresc.
First one kiss, then one more let us be lov - ers.
f

ritard.
a tempo, animato
Just once more. You and I, I and you, la la la la — la,
rit.
Just once more You and I, I and you, la la la la — la,
Just once more You and I, I and you, la la la la — la,
Just once more You and I, I and you, la la la la — la,
Just once more You and I, I and you, la la la,
Just once more You and I, I and you, la la la la — la,
Just once more. You and I, I and you, la la la la — la,
Just once more. You and I, I and you, la la la,
p rit.
Kiss me, sweetheart, kiss me, kiss me, sweetheart, la la la la — la,
Kiss me, sweetheart, kiss me, kiss me, sweetheart, la la la la — la,
Kiss me, sweetheart, kiss me, kiss me, sweetheart, la la la,
ritard.
a tempo, animato

p cresc.
You and I, I and you, la la la la — la, You and I, I and you, la la la la — la,
You and I, I and you, la la la la — la, You and I, I and you, la la la la — la,
You and I, I and you, la la la la — la, You and I, I and you, la la la la — la,
You and I, I and you, la la la la la, You and I, I and you, la la la la — la,
You and I, I and you, la la la la la. You and I, I and you. la la la,
You and I, I and you, la la la la — la. You and I, I and you, la la la la — la,
You and I, I and you, la al la la la, You and I, I and you, la la la la — la,
You and I, I and you, la la la la la. You and I, I and you, la la la,
la la la la la la la la — la la la la la la la la la — la,
la la la la la la la la la la la la la, la la la la — la,
la la la la la la la la la la la la la la la la,
mf

Più lento

acceler. e cresc.

you, you, you, you, you, you you, you, la – la la – la la – la la – la la —

acceler. e cresc.

you, you, you, you, you, you you, you, la – la la – la la – la la – la la —

acceler. e cresc.

you, you, you, you, you, you, you, you, la – la la – la la – la la – la la —

acceler. e cresc.

you, you, you, you, you, you, you, you, la – la la – la la – la la – la la —

acceler. e cresc.

you, you, you, you, you, you, you, you la – la la – la la – la la – la la —

acceler. e cresc.

you, you, you, you, you, you, you, you, la – la la – la la – la la – la la —

acceler. e cresc.

you, you, you, you, you, you, you, you, la – la la – la la – la la – la la —

acceler. e cresc.

you, you, you, you, you, you, you, you, la – la la – la la – la la – la la —

acceler. e cresc.

you, you, you, you, you, you, you, you, la – la la – la la – la la – la la —

acceler. e cresc.

you, you, you, you, you, you, you, you, la la la la la la la la la la la

acceler. e cresc.

you, you, you, you, you, you, you, you, la la la la la la la la la la la

Più lento

accel. e cresc.

— la la la — la la! —
— la la la — la la! —
— la la la — la la! —
— la la la — la la! —
— la la la — la la! —
— la la la — la la! —
— la la la — la la! —
— la la la — la la! —
— la la la — la la! —
la la — la la! —
la la — la la! —

BALLET

fz
p
fz
p
cresc.
Allegro
f
Allegretto
(Scottish)
p
mf

Allegretto molto moderato
(Russian)
f
mf
fz

fz
Tempo di Polka
SOPR.
ALT.
Come on, my darling, dance with me and
TEN.
BASS
CHORUS
Tempo di Polka
(Bohemian)
f
p
pp

trip the Pol - ka mer-ri-ly, while fiddlers gaily bow the strings, and ev - 'ry - body
laughs and sings. Come on, my dar - ling, dance with me and trip the Pol - ka
mer - ri - ly, while fid-dlers gaily bow the strings, and ev-'ry -body laughs and sings!

Take your partner by the hand, stamp-ing, hop-ping, nev-er stopping There's no better

mu-sic band an-y-where in all the land! Come

p p pp

on, my dar-ling, dance with me and trip the Pol-ka mer-ri-ly, while fid-dlers gai-ly

bow the strings, and ev-'ry-body laughs and sings! Come on my darling, dance with me and

trip the Pol - ka mer - ri - ly, while fid - dlers gai - ly bow the strings, and
ev - 'ry - body laughs and sings!
Allegro maestoso
(Hungarian)

fz
p
fz
fz
f
rit.
Allegro vivo
p
f
p
f
p
f
p
f
fz

f
p
Più Allegro
p
cresc.
f
f
ff

ORLOFSKY
a piacere
Tempo di Valse
Enough, my friends, e-nough! — You may cease this mer-ry
Tempo di Valse
PIANO
mf
f
dance, —
With ju- bi-lant sing-ing let
fz
fz
glass-es be cling-ing, and we our - selves be - gin to dance.
CHORUS
f
Yes, yes, a dance, a rol-lick-ing dance! Let's all be-
f
On with the dance, — with the dance! — Let us all be-
f
On with the dance, — with the dance! — Let us all be-

-gin to dance!
(All arrange for the waltz)
-gin to dance!
-gin to dance!
ff
SALLY, ROSALINDA, ADELE
f
Ah, hap-py day of di-vine de-light!
ORLOFSKY
Ah, hap-py day of di-vine de-light!
EISENSTEIN
Ah, hap-py day of di-vine de-light!
2 TENORS
FALKE, FRANK
Ah, hap-py day of di-vine de-light!
2 BASSES
Ah, hap-py day of di-vine de-light!
CHORUS
Ah, hap-py day of di-vine de-light!
Ah, hap-py day of di-vine de-light!
Ah, hap-py day of di-vine de-light!

ALL SOLOISTS AND CHORUS
Love and champagne banish care from sight. Could we live on as we do to-
Love and champagne banish care from sight. Could we live on as we do to-
Love and champagne banish care from sight. Could we live on as we do to-
night, life would for-ev er be gay and bright.
(Eisenstein and Frank, waltzing, meet each other)
night, life would for - ev - er be gay and bright.
night, life would for - ev - er be gay and bright.
pp
EISENSTEIN (E. supporting himself on Frank)
You are all I have on earth!
FRANK
You are my on - ly sal - vation.
ROSALINDA
When you meet in jail a - gain, how fun - ny a
ORLOFSKY
When you meet in jail a - gain, how fun - ny a
FALKE
When you meet in jail a - gain, how fun - ny a

ALL SOLOISTS AND CHORUS
sit - u - a-tion.
Ah, happy day of divine de-
sit - u - a-tion.
Ah, happy day of divine de-
sit - u - a-tion.
Ah, happy day of divine decresc.
-light! Love and champagne banish care from sight. Could we live on as we
-light! Love and champagne banish care from sight. Could we live on as we
-light! Love and champagne banish care from sight. Could we live on as we
do to-night, life would for-ev - er be gay and bright.
do to-night, life would for-ev - er be gay and bright.
do to-night, life would for-ev - er be gay and bright.

FRANK (to Eisenstein)
Brother, brother, my watch is slow; tell me what time it is.
pp
EISENSTEIN (looking for his watch)
Brother, mine also does not go, for it is already gone.
(to Rosal.)
Charming lady, I am asking,
pp
would you mind unmasking, let me see whom I adore,
and who stole my watch before?
ROSALINDA (grasping his hand)
pp

(drawing him forward confidentially)
ROSALINDA
My friend, do not ask what I con - ceal, the shock you would get would make you reel.
pp
ADELE, ORLOFSKY, AND SALLY
Ha ha ha ha, she is no fool, in - deed, she's no - bo - dy's fool!
EISENSTEIN
Hu hu hu hu, you are too cruel, you are too cruel.
ADELE
Are you a -
SOLOISTS AND CHORUS
In - deed, she's no - bo - dy's fool!
In - deed, she's no - bo - dy's fool!
she's no - bo - dy's fool!
cresc.
f p

SALLY
-fraid? Then go a - head! Perhaps she will weaken, if you are
CHORUS
Go a-head! Go a-head!
Go a-head! Go a-
Go a-head! Go a-
EISENSTEIN
clev-er. It has to be now or nev-er. Dar-ling, do not
-head!
-head!
ROSALINDA
hide from me. There's a freckle on my nose, there-fore
EISENSTEIN
dolce
I must hide my face. Such a freck-le can-not be!
dolce

ADELE, ORLOFSKY, AND SALLY
That dis - turbs him no de - gree.
FALKE, FRANK
That dis - turbs him no de - gree.
EISENSTEIN
No, your face I have to see!
Yes, her face he has to see!
Yes, her face he has to see!
(Eisenstein pursues Rosalinda)
cresc.
EISENSTEIN, FRANK (Counting)
(The clock strikes)
fz
One,
(more and more anxious)
two, three, four, five,

Più mosso
EISENSTEIN (startled)
FRANK (also)
six. Where's my hat? Where's my coat? It is ver-y late, Where's my hat? Where's my coat? It is
Più mosso
fz
very late.
SOLOISTS AND CHORUS
They are looking for
Bring his hat, bring his coat, O don't make him wait!
Bring his hat, bring his coat, O don't make him wait!
Bring his hat, bring his coat, O don't make him wait!
mf
FRANK
FRANK, EISENSTEIN
ff
me! And I know where I should be! Where's my hat? Where's my coat? O give me my
fz

(Servants bring various coats and hats which do not fit)
coat!
f acceler.
Bring his coat, bring his hat, bring his coat, ha ha ha, bring his hat, O bring him his
f
Bring his coat, bring his hat, bring his coat, ha ha ha, bring his hat, O bring him his
f
Bring his coat, bring his hat, bring his coat, ha ha ha, bring his hat, O bring him his
ff acceler.
FRANK (leaning on Eisenstein)
EISENSTEIN
Dear Marquis, I hope you will call on me. Yes, in-
coat, ha ha ha!
coat, ha ha ha!
coat, ha ha ha!
pp
ADELE, SALLY
ORLOFSKY
Good-bye, good-bye, ha ha!
FALKE
Good-bye, good-bye, ha ha!
EISENSTEIN
EISENSTEIN, FRANK
-deed, the moment my time is free. Let's say good-bye.

ff
Ah, hap-py day of di-vine de-light! Love and cham-
Ah, hap-py day of di-vine de-light! Love and cham-
Ah, hap-py day of di-vine de-light! Love and cham-
ROSALINDA, ADELE, ORLOFSKY, AND SALLY
-pagne ban-ish care from sight. Could we live on as we do to-
-pagne ban-ish care from sight. Could we live on as we do to-
-pagne ban-ish care from sight. Could we live on as we do to-
-pagne ban-ish care from sight. Could we live on as we do to-
Allegro
-night, la la
-night, then life would be for-ev-er gay and
-night, then life would be for-ev-er gay and
-night, then life would be for-ev-er gay and-
Allegro
ff
p
cresc.

la la la la la la la!
bright, then life would be for - ev — er gay and bright.
bright, then life would be for - ev — er gay and bright.
bright, then life would be for - ev — er gay and bright.
(Eisenstein and Frank, dancing the last tempo, move, staggering, arm in arm toward the background
They are surrounded by the dancers, while the curtain falls.)

End of Act II

Act III

No. 12. Entr'acte

f
f
con forza
ff
ff

No. 13. Melodrama

Frank

Moderato
(Frank appears, his overcoat
PIANO
pp

awry, his hat pressed down deep over his eyes. He staggers and tries in vain to walk steadily.

Coming forward, he takes off his hat and tosses it into a corner.)

Tempo di valse
(He begins quietly to move in time to the music
acceler.
ritard.
mf
pp

and whistles to himself)
(whistled)
(He becomes more and more lively and
pp

waltzes with his half-removed overcoat. Suddenly he stops . . . .

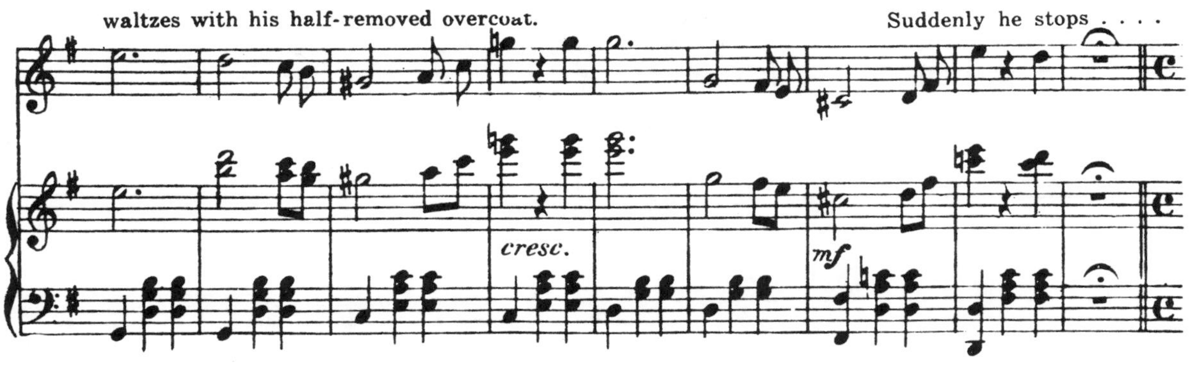

Tempo di marcia moderato

remembering where he is, he pulls himself together, makes an effort to be serious and tries

again to take off his overcoat . . . . finally succeeding.

Waltz His high spirits gain the upper hand again. He thinks he is in the ballroom, makes

several bows and mumbles: "Tanja, come here . Sally, too! I like you! . ." He turns towards

the other side and speaks with a heavy tongue: "Marquis, give me your hand, be my friend." . .)

Allegretto
(sings first softly, humming to himself, then increasingly louder.)
His maj - es - ty we cele - brate, cel - e - brate, long and late,
joy - ous - ly to - geth - er. We toast Champagne, the Great! A toast to Champagne, the great mon— Pst!
G.P.
p
pp
f
lento
Polka un poco moderato
(looks around, frightened, to see if anyone has heard him and tries to appear steady on his feet.)
(He notices the tea-things on the table in the back, and goes toward them. He carries them, staggering, and with great effort to the table in the foreground, lights the oil lamp after a few comic attempts. He is very warm. He fans himself and drinks a glass of water.)
mf
1.
2.

(Sinks exhausted into a chair,
Meno mosso
p rit.
grasps a newspaper and tries to read, but his thoughts still fly to the dance.)
Waltz, più moderato
pp
(He whistles, falling asleep.)
(Lets the newspaper fall!)
ppp
(whistled)
and goes to sleep.)
ppp
riten.
Più lento
smorz.

No. 14. Couplets

do— as the shy in-gé-nue: I sing and dance and wave my fan, and in the
pp
end, I get my man. He says to me "Let's take a walk." He holds my hand, we
p
hard-ly talk. We wan-der slow-ly through the park. The lights fade out, the stage is dark..
La a la la la la la la la la la la la la la la la la la la la la
la la la la la la la la la— la— la!— If you
rit.
ppp
rit.

138
Meno mosso
ten.
più ani-
saw the way I can act and play, the fact is ab - so - lute - ly clear, That a
cresc.
colla parte
p più ani-
mato
girl like me, a girl like me was born for a stage ca - reer.
mato
rit.
rit.
f animato
Tempo di marcia
When I play Madame Pompadour I
p
do it with "l'a-mour, l'a-mour." Smil - ing here and greeting there, I
run, ah, each lit - tle state af - fair. I have a mink and an
p
42609

er - mine of my own. I'm the pow'r be- - - hind the throne.
fz
fz
Proud and stately,— dig - ni - fied, se - rene, I am ev - 'ry inch a queen.
cresc.
p
La — la — la la la la la la la la. la —
SALLY (imitating a trumpet)
Tra ta ta ta ta ta tra ta ta ta ta ta tra ta ta ta ta ta
FRANK (imitating a drum)
Rem pem plem prrrrrr rem pem plem prrrrrr rem pem plem prrrrrrr
fz
cresc.
la la la la — la — la la la la
tra ta ta ta ta ta tra ta ta ta ta ta tra ta ta ta ta ta
rem pem plem prrrrrr rem pem plem prrrrrrr rem pem plem prrrrrrr
fz
cresc.

la la la la! If you
tra ta ta ta ta ta tra ta ta ta ta ta!
rem pem plem prrrrrrrrrrr rem prrrrrr rem pem plem!
p
Meno mosso
saw the way I can act and play, the fact is ab-so-lute-ly
cresc.
ten.
più animato
clear That a girl like me, a girl like me was
colla parte
p più animato
rit.
born for a stage ca-reer.
animato
rit.
f

Allegretto grazioso
I play a young Par-is-ian wife, ah ah
pp
Who's rath-er bored with mar-ried life, ah ah
My hus-band is an old Mar-
-quis, ah ah who can-not quite keep up with
me. Ah!
f
p
I meet a
fz
p

handsome count one day, We fall in love and run a - way. In time the count betrays me
too. O — Lord, I — don't know_ what to do! Ah! —
cresc.
mf
lento a piacere
Act III: My lov - ing husband calls, Ah! —
p
— I shoot them both, the curtain falls! Ah, — ah,
ad lib.
colla parte
Più mosso
yes!

No. 15. Trio

Rosalinda, Alfred, and Eisenstein

EISENSTEIN: *Do they look guilty, and will I trap them!*

We can't make demands, we are in his hands. We
make a con - fession? We can't make demands, we are in his hands. We
force a con - fession? They can't make demands, they are in my hands. They
Allegro non troppo
are in his hands, we can't make de - mands!
are in his hands, we can't make de - mands!
can't make de - mands! no, they can't make de - mands!
Allegro non troppo
EISENSTEIN
Now please de-scribe the sit - u -
- a - tion, pre - cise - ly, all re - veal - ing, not e - ven one de - tail con -

ROSALINDA

-ceal - ing, and meanwhile I shall take no - ta - tion. The case is rath - er

ALFRED

cur - ious, you must employ your wit! It real - ly makes me fur - ious; that much I must ad-

EISENSTEIN

- mit. All right, then, f-f-furnish me with good pre-tense on which to base your whole de -

f

p

- fense!

acceler.

fz *f*

ALFRED

Last

ff

Allegretto
night I had ad-ven-tures of most pe-cu-liar kind. While with this charming
la-dy, in pri-va-cy I dined, by mis-take I was ar-rest-ed and
here in jail con-fined.
(astonished)
Now
EISENSTEIN
(roughly)
You got what you de-serve, you had an aw-ful nerve.
what on earth is that you say? Your task is to de-fend me.
Ex-cuse the tem-per

ROSALINDA
ALFRED
EISENSTEIN
p dolce
poco rit.
I dis - play, my sub - ject car - ries me a - way. I nev - er would of -
poco rit.
fz
p
a tempo
fend you, no, my task is to de - fend you.
a tempo
p
p
p
I find it queer that you ap - pear in
I find it queer that you ap - pear in
such a rude and an - - gry mood. You must be calm at
such a rude and an - - gry mood. You must be calm at
(to himself)
The fact is clear that things don't look so ver - y good. I must be calm at
poco rit.
poco rit.

a tempo
poco animato
pp
an-y cost or else we both are lost. You must be calm
pp
an-y cost or else we both are lost. You must be calm
pp
an-y cost or else my case is lost. I must be calm
a tempo
poco animato
pp
Tempo I
p
or we're lost. It all was ver-y harmless, and noth-ing bad took
or we're lost.
or I'm lost.
Tempo I
p
pp
place, But if the tale were ru-mored I could not show my face. My
EISENSTEIN (breaking out)
f
hus-band would most surely blame me for this dis-grace. And he would be cor-

ROSALINDA
(astonished)
Now what on earth is that you say? Your
-rect, your con-duct was ab - ject.
task is to de - fend me!
(collecting himself)
Ex - cuse the tem - per I dis - play, my
p
fz
p
p dolce
poco rit.
subject car - ries me a - way. I nev - er would of - fend you, no, my
poco rit.
fz
p
p
ROSALINDA
p
I find it queer that you ap - pear in
ALFRED
p
I find it queer that you ap - pear in
a tempo
task is to de - fend you.
a tempo

poco rit.
such a rude and an - gry mood. You must be calm at
such a rude and an gry mood. You must be calm at
(to himself)
The fact is clear that things don't look so ver - y good. I must be calm at
poco rit.
a tempo
poco animato
pp
an - y cost or else we both are lost. You must be calm
pp
an - y cost or else we both are lost. You must be calm
pp
an - y cost or else my case is lost. I must be calm
a tempo
poco animato
pp
Un poco meno mosso
or we're lost!
or we're lost!
(with snarling tone)
or I'm lost! I beg you to re-view the case, each
Un poco meno mosso
p
f

string.
ff
in-stant to re-trace, No smallest de-tail to e-rase. Did nothing else take
p
f
p string.
f
a tempo, con moto
ALFRED
ROSALINDA
EISENSTEIN
place? These questions are beside the point! What's that? Let's
a tempo, con moto
p
cresc.
ROSALINDA
talk about our case. Did nothing else take place? But, sir, what do you
f
EISENSTEIN
think of me? Your point I real-ly fail to see. De-scribe your full im-pression! Did
più f
ff a piacere
nothing else take place? I need a full con-fes-sion, I need a full con-
acceler.
fz colla parte

ROSAL.
a tempo
How dare you!
How dare you!
It
ALFRED
How dare you!
-fes-sion.
a tempo
Allegretto moderato
ROSAL.
al-most seems as if you tried to rep-re-sent my husband's side,
but now I shall in-dict him. The shameless monster was un-true! And
there is noth-ing I won't do to pay him back in kind and fight him.

poco animato
Last night he went to a soi - rée and flirted with a whole ballet.
To leave they had to force him, to force him! When
rit.
pp
a tempo
he comes home, the horrid brute. he will receive a nice sur - prise! I'll
fz
p
Poco più
give that monster two black eyes and then, and then I shall di -
f
- vorce him, I will give that monster two black eyes and then divorce
cresc.

pp
him! I'll give that mon - ster two black eyes and then, and
She'll give that mon - ster two black eyes and then she will di -
She'll give that mon - ster two black eyes and then she will di -
mf
f
then I shall di - vorce him! I will give that mon - ster two black eyes and
vorce him, then she will di - vorce him! She'll give that monster two black
- vorce him, then she will di - vorce him! She'll give that monster two black
cresc.
ril.
then di - vorce him!
eyes, and then, then she will di - vorce him!
eyes and then, and then, and then she will di - vorce him!
ff

Allegro non troppo
ALFRED
Now that all is known to you, tell us quick-ly
what to do. Can you give us some ad-vice, cure the sin-ner of his vice, make the
ALFRED
husband pay the price? Have you gone mad?
EISENSTEIN (pounding the table)
I've hea d e-nough! Your time is
ROSALINDA
Are you in-sane? What does this lan-guage mean?
ALFRED
What does this lan-guage mean?
EISENSTEIN
(with ominous voice)
up! Trans-

Recitative
- gres - - sors, taste my fu - ry, at last vengeance is mine! You
trem.
ff
a tempo
His name is
His name is
(throwing aside his wig and glasses)
stand before your ju - ry, my name is Ei - sen-stein!
fz
a tempo
ff
Ei - sen-stein! His name is Eisenstein!
Ei - sen-stein! His name is Eisenstein!
Yes! Yes!
p
cresc. e acceler.
Più mosso
I'm the one who was mis - treated. You're the one who lied and cheated.
fz

cresc.

But at last you see the dawn of Judg - - ment Day!

cresc.

ROS. *f* You're the one who lied an cheated. I'm the one who was mis - treated,

AD. *f* You're the one who lied and cheated. I'm the one who was mis - treated,

EIS. *f* You're the one who lied and cheated. I'm the one who was mis - treated.

ff

cresc. *f* *p*

now you try to put the blame on me. Ei - sen - stein

cresc. *f* *p*

now you try to put the blame on me. This Ei - sen - stein!

cresc. *f* *p*

now you try to put the blame on me. This Ei - sen - stein!

p cresc. *p* *mf*

must re - sign! Eisenstein must pay the fine. *ff* Ven - - - geance!

This Ei - sen - stein will not de - cline. *ff* Ven - - - geance!

This Ei - sen - stein will not de - cline. *ff* Ven - - - geance!

p *mf* *p* *ff*

Come, re - sign, oh, Ei - sen - stein! Pay the fine, oh, Ei - sen - stein. Ven - - - - - - - geance now is mine! Pray hear me out un - til the end!
This Ei - sen - stein! This Ei - sen-stein. Re-venge now is mine! Don't
This Ei - sen - stein! This Ei - sen-stein. Re-venge will now be mine!
mf
cresc.
ff
ALFRED
jump at false con - clusions, friend!
EISENSTEIN
How dare you stand and call me down, while you have on my

ROSALINDA
Too bad it was so good a
dres - sing gown!
ALFRED
This is your bath-robe, I ad - mit.
ff
fit!
EISENSTEIN
This proof they can't re - fute, and they both turn pale and mute.
You're the one who lied and cheated. I'm the one who was mis - treat - ed.
You're the one who lied and cheated. I'm the one who was mis - treat - ed.
You're the one who lied and cheated. I'm the one who was mis - treat - ed.
ff

cresc.
Then he rag - es: - vengeance I shall take.
Ei - sen - stein
So their scores an - e - qual to - tal make.
This Ei - senstein!
But just wait, for vengeance I shall take.
This Ei - sen - stein!
p
cresc.
mf
must re - sign.
Eisenstein must pay the fine, ven - - - geance, come resign, oh,
This Eisenstein will not decline. Ven - - - geance, oh,
This Eisenstein will not decline. Ven - - - geance, oh,
ff
Ei - sen - stein, pay the fine, oh, Ei - sen - stein, ven - - - - - geance now is
Ei - sen-stein will not de - cline, re - venge will now be
Ei - sen-stein will not de - cline, - venge will now be

Più presto

fz

mine, Ven - - - geance is mine, ven - - - - geance is

mine Ven - - - - geance is mine, ven - - - - geance is

mine, Ven - - - geance is mine, ven - - - - geance is

Più presto

fz *fz*

mine! Ve ve ve ve ve ve ve ven - - - - - geance is

mine! Ve ve ve ve ve ve ve ven - - - - - geance is

mine! Ve ve ve ve ve ve ve ven - - - - geance is

ff

mine! ______

mine! ______

mine! ______

ff

Ped. *

No. 16. Finale of Act III

Full Company

TUTTI
braggart with his master wit has fal - len in the pit.
EISENSTEIN
braggart with his master wit has fal - len in the pit. Won't you tell me out and
braggart with his master wit has fal - len in the pit.
out what is this sto - ry all a - bout? And what are you driving at? It's the
FALKE
FALKE
ven- geance of the Bat! Yes, the vengeance of the Bat!
Yes, the vengeance of the Bat! But the
TUTTI
Yes, the vengeance of the Bat! But the
Yes, the vengeance of the Bat! But the

joke you played with such a bang turned out to be a boom-e-rang. This time it was the
joke you played with such a bang turned out to be a boom-e-rang. This time it was the
joke you played with such a bang turned out to be a boom-e-rang. This time it was the
clev-er Bat who gave you tit for tat!
EISENSTEIN
clev-er Bat who gave you tit for tat! Do explain it
clev-er Bat who gave you tit for tat!
f
p grazioso.
FALKE
from the start. All the an-guish you went through was a joke I played on
cresc.

ORLOFSKY
FALKE
TUTTI
Was a joke he played on you.
EISENSTEIN
I played my part.
you!
Was a joke he played on you.
And the prince?
And A-
Was a joke he played on you.
ADELE
ROSALINDA
With all my heart.
Stage con-
EISENSTEIN
(to Alfred)
ALFRED
EISENSTEIN (to Ros.)
-dele?
But your dinner? A mere in-vention. But my houserobe?
-ven-tion.
EISENSTEIN
That is won-der-ful! Oh, bless you. Oh, how glad I am to know. Come, dear
ALFRED (softly to Orlofsky)
wife, let me ca-ress you!
It was not ex-act-ly so, why

ADELE
should we start con - fu - sion and end his fond il - lu - sion. Well, and
cresc.
fz p
what becomes of me?
FRANK
To this jail you have the key; as a
mp
fa - ther would ap - proach you, for the thea - ter I shall coach you. I'm a
ORLOFSKY
(Taking Adele's arm.)
f
Un poco meno
pa - tron of the arts: I will spon - sor her de - but. It is Or - lofsky's
rit.
a tempo
mp
p
mot - to, "cha - cun, à son gôut." It is Or - lofsky's motto, "chacun à son gôut."
It is Or - lofsky's motto, "chacun à son gôut."
TUTTI
EISENST. (spoken)
Rosalinda, forgive your faithful Gabriel! You see, the champagne alone was to blame.
It is Or - lofsky's motto, "chacun à son gôut."
It is Or - lofsky's motto, "chacun à son gôut."
f
trem.

Allegro non troppo
ROSALINDA
Champagne's de - li - cious bubbles, tra-la la la la la
la la, scattered all our troubles, la la la la la la la, — it taught me something
price - less; that husbands are not vice - less. A wife must be resourceful to make a man re -
- morse-ful. We toast Cham - pagne, the essence of the es-sence, the King of Ef - fer -
vescence, the King of Ef fer-vescence A toast, a toast, a toast! His
TUTTI
A toast, a toast, a toast!
A toast, a toast, a toast!
A toast, a toast, a toast!

End of Operetta